A Finnish Christmas

A
Finnish Christmas Cookbook

Recipes and Traditions from the Old Country

Sargit Warriner
and
Liisa Krumsieg

NORTH STAR PRESS OF ST. CLOUD, INC.

Color photography by Edward J. Purcell,
Architectural Photo Studios, Milwaukee, Wisconsin.

Drawings by graphic artist Jeremy Anacher
and by Fred Krumsieg and Sargit Warriner.

Copyright © 1999 Sargit Warriner and Liisa Krumsieg

First Edition, September 1999

Second Edition, June 2001

Third Edition, November 2003

ISBN: 0-87839-133-9

Printed in the United States of America by
Versa Press, Inc., East Peoria, Illinois.

Published by
North Star Press of St. Cloud, Inc.
PO Box 451
St. Cloud, MN 56302

This book is dedicated to our children

Annette
Ina
Karl
Kirsti

Acknowledgements

We would like to thank friends and family members who helped in testing many of the recipes presented here. We are especially grateful to our husbands, Read Warriner and Fred Krumsieg. Without their contributions and support, it would have been impossible to complete this book. We also would like to thank Majlis Wassholm and Ingeborg Sunstrom.

The Authors

Contents

Introduction

Although the Christmas of our imagination is often a picture-perfect, snow-covered, peaceful rural scene, today's Finnish Christmas celebration mainly comes from genteel customs that evolved in city life and gradually spread to all parts of the country during the past one hundred years. The Christmas Eve we actually create, whatever its shortcomings when compared to the ideal, will have strong connections to the traditions in each of our own families. These shared traditions and good feelings are common threads that stay in our memories from childhood. As in earlier times, certain Finnish Christmas Eve traditions, such as the Christmas sauna and visits to family gravesites in nearby cemeteries, are often still observed. Nevertheless, a fundamental part of the celebration in Finland, as in many nations, is the food preparation that creates a special aroma of Christmas that lingers first in the kitchen and then gradually settles in the dining area as the dishes are carried in for the dinner.

The Christmas Eve of the authors' childhood, with all the activities and marvelous, traditional food seems very close in time. In reality, it is a long time since all the family members and friends have gathered around a common table. But each new Christmas celebrated with family and friends of today is an opportunity to reach back in our minds to the warmth and happiness of those times. For one author, this has been the time to open the old red folder, on which an angel was pasted years ago, to take out recipes that were handwritten by family members and friends and placed alongside notes of news and Merry Christmas wishes. These recipes are part of family Christmases and include all the rich ingredients used in traditional cooking methods.

The purpose of this book is to give the reader an intimate glimpse of Christmas traditions in Finland with some historic background material. It also tells how customs have changed in modern times to include features that may not be authentically Finnish but are now unquestionably a part of Finnish Christmases. The authors, however, have tried throughout carefully to follow the authentic food traditions in order to convey to the readers an understanding of how these special dishes have remained so important at this season.

Whatever one's own Christmas customs and however much they have departed from the old Finnish ways, it is the food, the ritual of food preparation, and finally the friends and family around the Christmas Eve dinner table with the blessings of Christmas peace, that make memorable the Christmas celebration. This is the traditional Finnish Christmas the authors hope to share with their readers.

Christmas peace
Joulurauhaa

Sargit Warriner
Liisa Krumsieg

A Finnish Christmas

Chapter One

Finnish Christmas in Earlier Times

The traditional Finnish Christmas celebration is a combination of ancient pagan fests and Scandinavian harvest festivals. It also has a great deal of cultural flavor imported from Germany and Sweden.

Up until the later part of the nineteenth century, most Finns, like other Scandinavians, supported themselves through agriculture. Fall was a busy time with harvesting, slaughtering, and hunting. Afterwards great preparations were made to celebrate the harvest and to bless the homestead in hopes of a fruitful new year. The feasting took place on calendar dates set in 300 A.D. by the Romans who decided that the equinox would divide the calendar into fall and spring seasons. This was the only time of the year when the continual work of the farming community could be interrupted for a period of time. It also happens to be the coldest and the darkest period in the North, and this made the celebrations especially important for keeping up the spirits of the people. The harvest feast was largely a collective celebration; then the emphasis on Christmas made it more of a family event.

The households in towns were similar to those of farmers in that they were also forced to be self-reliant for their food supply during the winter months. Consequently, Christmas preparations started early in the fall at the time of the harvest. Pantry shelves were filled with preserved berries and pickled vegetables in glass jars. Cold cellars were cleaned for the new crops of potatoes, root vegetables, and dried fish.

In Germany, it had been a custom since 1600 to bring an evergreen inside the house. An evergreen was considered a symbol of good luck and fertility; it was part of the harvest decorations. In parts of Finland, it had been a centuries-old custom to raise a tree and decorate it outdoors to solemnize a wedding or to celebrate

Midsummer. Also, it was customary to bring a small evergreen indoors to celebrate a person's name day. The tree was set on a table and decorated with small presents. This was done long before the idea of a Christmas tree came from Germany to Finland.

City people, who were often exposed to ideas from a wider area, first heard about the German custom and brought evergreen trees inside their homes for their own Christmas celebrations. In 1829, the first Christmas tree known to be in a private residence appeared in a wealthy merchant's home in Helsinki. He supposedly had eight of them. In those years, a family in the city got their tree through the generosity of their friends or relatives living in the countryside who selected the tree, always a spruce, and brought it to town. Much time was devoted to finding the most perfectly shaped tree. When a tree was chosen, it was marked in the fall to be cut down on Christmas Eve and brought to the house on a horse-drawn sleigh.

Gradually, the tree was also adopted in the farming community's Christmas celebrations. When a tree was brought into the home, it was hung from the ceiling, which certainly made it impossible for the tree to fall over. Later, Christmas tree stands were used to keep the tree upright, thus allowing the tree to stand straight visually regardless of weight distribution. Tree stands were typically handmade of two pieces of wood affixed in a cross formation. The trunk of the tree was pushed into a hole bored into the center of the stand. Since the tree was always freshly cut and not brought into the house until Christmas Eve, watering was not a problem.

The trees in the homes of the wealthy were grander than the trees in the working-class homes, but the excitement involved in decoration was common to both. Countless hours were spent making paper chains and cutting out paper angels and stars. A decoration at the top of the tree was not used at first. However, later, again as a result of German influence, an angel and a star were alternated in this honored place. Fruits, such as apples and raisins, were hung on the tree from strings, and plain cotton balls were spread on the branches. With time, the fresh apples disappeared, and wooden ones came into use. Home-baked ginger hearts and stars, hung on the branches with ribbon or string, were especially important to the young members of the family, who would be permitted to eat these treats when the tree was taken down. Later, a silk band, with religious messages printed or hand sewn on it, was wrapped around the tree. The band symbolized continuity of life. Hand-dipped candles were tied with string between branches until a special candleholder became commercially available. Some families bought electric candle strings from the store when they first appeared in 1930. Shine and glitter were added to the Christmas tree when gold and silver threads were applied to commercially made decorations. About 1924, the first Christmas decorations were produced in Finland by Weiste Manufacturing Company in Pukinmäki, a small village located just outside Helsinki. As a child, the author had the opportunity to tour the premises, and she remembers the pleasure and excitement of seeing the glittering angels and stars packed in boxes and observing the spinning of the gold and silver threads onto large spools.

In the merchant's home, the Christmas tree was placed in the living room behind closed doors and decorated on Christmas Eve. Family members put on their best suits and Sunday dresses for the occasion. Then the doors were opened, and children and adults joined in admiring the sight of the tree with live candles burning on the branches. The wonderful aroma of warm, melting candle wax mixed with the fresh fragrance of the evergreen and filled the room.

As mentioned earlier, the Christmas tree was slowly gaining popularity in farmhouses. In the country, the old way of celebrating Christmas Eve included a thorough scrubbing and cleaning of both the dwelling and the barns. Fresh, good smelling straw was given to the animals as bedding, and some of it was brought into the house and put on the floor where later in the evening different games were played. Living candles gave a gleam to the straw. A white linen tablecloth was spread over the table, and a freshly baked loaf of bread with straw decorations was set in the middle of the table. Delicious food was brought in for the festive meal, and all the family gathered around the table and joined in the Christmas spirit.

Chapter Two

Santa Lucia Day

Who is Santa Lucia? According to legend, Lucia was a pious peasant girl from Italy who was one of the first Christians to be persecuted and became an early Christian saint. In Sweden, the tradition of celebrating Santa Lucia Day goes back almost two hundred years. The Swedes adopted Santa Lucia as a symbol of light, purity, and generosity and created a Santa Lucia pageant that takes place during the darkest time of the year.

There are a number of legends about Santa Lucia; the following is one of them. It tells us that she was a beautiful Italian peasant girl living with her mother, who fell very ill. As a Christian, Lucia did good works and offered prayers on behalf of her mother who recovered miraculously. However, the young girl's fiancé, a pagan, objected to her behavior and became angry with her on account of her good deeds. According to the legend, he had her killed.

In Finland, 1930 was the first year that Finns whose mother tongue was Swedish (about six percent of the population) arranged a Santa Lucia Day pageant that was held outdoors in Helsinki. This Lucia pageant gave the large audience an understanding of their interwoven cultural heritage shared with Sweden. Today, Santa Lucia Day is celebrated on December 13, which marks the beginning of the Christmas season in Sweden.

Deep economic depression in the thirties and during the war years led to the abandonment of the Santa Lucia parade in Helsinki until 1949. At that time, the Swedish-language newspaper, *Huvudstadsbladet*, and organizations especially supporting the Swedish-speaking population reawakened interest in Lucia Day. Since the 1950s, this pageant has been part of the Christmas tradition for the Swedish speaking Finns, especially in Helsinki and the coastal towns. Today, the Finnish-speaking Finns have also adopted Santa Lucia pageants, which are gaining popularity throughout the country.

In the home, this celebration takes on a charming character. A young daughter of the family, representing Lucia, is dressed in a white gown. Around her waist she wears a red ribbon and on her head a wreath, traditionally made from lingonberry branches, that has four lighted candles inserted in it. Santa Lucia carries a tray with coffee, saffron bread, and gingerbread cookies to her family to awaken them for breakfast while singing Lucia's song about a miracle bringing back light.

Saffron Bread
Sahramileipä

2   cups lukewarm milk
2   ounces fresh yeast or 2 packages of dry yeast
½   teaspoon powdered saffron
1   tablespoon cognac (optional)
½   cup butter at room temperature
½   teaspoon salt
½   cup sugar
½   cup raisins
6   cups flour (approximately)
1   egg, lightly beaten, for glazing

In a bowl, dissolve the fresh yeast in a couple of tablespoons of lukewarm water. Set aside. When the yeast has become active, add the lukewarm milk, sugar, cognac, and salt to the yeast. Stir in the flour, one cup at a time. Knead until the dough is smooth. Let the covered dough rise in a warm place until it doubles in size (about an hour). Punch down and work in the butter, raisins, and the saffron. Turn the dough onto a lightly floured board and knead the dough to be sure it is smooth. Form the dough into shapes such as those shown on page 51. Let them rise in a warm place about 30 minutes, and then glaze the top with egg. Bake about 20 to 25 minutes at 400° F.

Saffron bread and the sweet bread have many traditional shapes. These breads can be baked into forms symbolic of the holidays. The shapes can represent the various themes of Christmas. For example, breads formed into certain shapes remind us of religious connections like the priest's hair, the Christmas star, the Christmas cross, a church door, or they can be formed into shapes connected to Lucia Day, such as a Lucia crown or a Lucia wheel.

Chapter Three

The Christmas Sauna

Since prehistoric times, the sauna has been part of the Finnish way of bathing and relaxing. In many Finnish families, it still is a tradition to go to sauna on Christmas Eve to relax and enjoy the pleasant scent of a switch of pliable birch twigs (*vihta*) filling the sauna room. The *vihta* is first dipped in a pail of cold water, then shaken over the hot stones, and then dipped again in the cold water. This treatment softens the *vihta* so that the bather can use it to gently beat his body and stimulate the skin. Sprinkling water over the hot stones brings a bracing wave of steam to the room, where the temperature can be 190 F, or higher, depending on the bather's tolerance for heat.

In the countryside, every individual home has a sauna, a small wooden building, often constructed as a separate building. If there is access to a lake on the property, the sauna will be standing only a few feet from the shoreline so that the bathers can swim, in winter or summer, directly from the sauna.

Since 1980, apartments in Finland have been constructed with an individual sauna for each living unit, even in the high-rise buildings. However, in older apartment buildings, there is usually one sauna unit shared by the residents. Located on the ground floor, it includes a dressing room, a room for showers, and the sauna section with different levels of benches and the hot stove, which now is usually electrically heated. The sauna is booked by the residents at regularly scheduled times for each family, so it is possible that one's "sauna hour" may not fall on Christmas Eve.

"*Terveiset saunasta*" is an old saying used to greet the other bathers who are dressed and ready for the "Sauna Coffee Table." However, some of the bathers might also like to have a glass of homemade beer, *Kotikalja*.

Homemade Beer
Kotikalja

1	gallon of water
1½	cups of rye malt flour
1	cup sugar
½	teaspoon of fresh yeast
1	small lemon, cut in quarters

Boil the water in a separate container and pour it over the combined sugar, rye malt flour, and lemon wedges. Let the mixture cool to a lukewarm temperature and then add the yeast. Let this liquid ferment at room temperature overnight. On the following day, strain it through a small net sieve and pour it into bottles that can be corked very tightly. Store the bottles in a cool place overnight. Serve the *kalja* the next day.

Chapter Four

The Coffee Table

The coffee table, or *kahvipäytä*, means the table set formally for serving coffee and light refreshments to guests. The table is set with beautiful linens and the best china with small silver coffee spoons. With the sugar bowl, there are special small tongs for the cubes. The cream pitcher is filled with real cream. The hostess pours the coffee in the cups and then invites the guests to the table. Now comes the real worry from the hostess' point of view. Which guest will feel he or she is of the correct age or rank to lead the procession? The old rule, especially in rural areas, was that if a minister was among the guests, custom dictated that he would be first at the coffee table, followed by the eldest lady. Often the coffee is cooling in the cups as the hostess again encourages the guests to come to the table, saying, "*kahvi on kaadettu*" (coffee is poured). If a guest jumps up immediately, it might show that he is hungry, and the coffee table is not a dinner table. After moments of hesitation, one of the guests may rise and say, "Well, no one seems ready to go first, so I'll have to." Everyone is very pleased to hear that announcement, and now all can join in the line to the coffee table. Of course, when the group consists only of family and very close friends, these unwritten rules are not observed, and the line to the table forms more naturally.

A guest will never take more than one or two items onto his plate, because in olden days doing so indicated that one did not have such treats at home—in other words, that one was poor or uncouth. Even today this perception lingers, and guests feel it is improper to fill their plates. The hostess then encourages her guests to return to the coffee table several times, and one is obliged to do so in order to please her. Coffee is served for each turn at the table. Even for small gatherings, the guests are expected to return to the living room with hot coffee and cakes as well as spoons, forks and napkins, performing an impressive balancing act in the process.

The popularity of this traditional coffee table has contributed to the fact that the Finns are among the greatest consumers of coffee in the world.

Chapter Five

The Christmas Holidays Today

For the Finns, the holiday season begins on the first Sunday in Advent with *"Pikkujoulu,"* Little Christmas. At church services, the hymn, "Hosanna" (*Hoosianna, Daavidin poika!*), by G.J. Vogler, is sung. The early Christmas celebration in businesses, schools, offices, and other groups is also referred to as *"Pikkujoulu."* Small gifts are often exchanged, and a little tree set on a table is decorated. A tradition that probably originated in Sweden around the turn of the century is the lighting of an additional candle on each Sunday of Advent until there are four burning on the last Sunday, indicating that Christmas has arrived.

Although commercially available gifts have been advertised in local newspapers since the 1800s, Christmas gifts traditionally remain homemade. Economic development prior to and following the Second World War was associated with the growth of shopping for holiday gift giving. Nowadays there is renewed interest in making Christmas gifts at home instead of buying them. These might be hand-woven tablecloths, intricate needlepoint, handmade lace, knitted mittens and scarves, hand-dipped candles, or small baskets made of birch bark. Homemade candies, jellies, and mustard are popular gifts. Gingerbread cookies, *pulla*—the Finnish sweet bread, and prune tarts are favorites from the oven for every family's coffee table.

The common use of straw for making decorations, such as stars, angels, and goats of various sizes, illustrates the close links between Christmas and the old harvest rituals. The handmade, geometric straw mobile, called a *Himmeli,* is a decoration that shows the skill of its maker. Constructing a *Himmeli* is not difficult, but, it is a slow process and demands concentration. Pieces of fresh straw are first cut to the exact lengths required, and then they are strung together to form a mobile. One needs three-dimensional visualization in order to put together the more complicated designs.

Hung from the ceiling and turning slowly in the candlelight, the *Himmeli* is one of the Finns' most cherished Christmas decorations. It is rich in tradition, structurally as uniform as a snowflake, but delicate, alive, and always changing. In the countryside, use of the *Himmeli* as the primary seasonal decoration goes back in time to before the use of the Christmas tree. It was almost forgotten until it was brought back to decorate Finnish homes in the 1940s, thanks to its active promotion by the Finnish press. There are varying opinions about the original meaning of *Himmeli.* Some researchers assume that it had something to do with forecasting the coming summer's crop. Others say that it might have been displayed as protection from evil spirits. Now, the *Himmeli* has no symbolic meaning except to beautify the home and to show off the skills of the maker.

Other decorations originating in the countryside are a wooden bird with widespread wings and the Thomas cross, *Tuomaan risti,* each very delicately carved from a single piece of wood. These are popular handmade items found across the country.

The short-stemmed, red Christmas tulip was used on Finnish Christmas tables in earlier times. The bulbs were imported from Holland. Beginning at the turn of century, the scent of hyacinths filled the rooms. Later, the lily-of-the-valley became very popular, especially in flower arrangements. Since the 1960s, poinsettias have gained popularity, though they actually had become available starting in the 1930s. Floral arrangements that include these living flowers in a variety of baskets are more common than cut flowers for use as gifts during the Christmas season.

When people in Finland talk about how they celebrate Christmas, they mean Christmas Eve rather than Christmas Day. The highlight is Christmas Eve, and the activities of that day are important for everyone, although they may differ somewhat from family to family.

Among the oldest legal documents in Scandinavia are the Ordinances of Peace. If one didn't follow these regulations, one could be severely punished. From the Ordinances of Peace arose the common practice in the larger towns of declaring Christmas Peace. Since the Middle Ages, the Finns have kept this custom alive in Turku, the old capital city of Finland. The proclamation is read in both Finnish and Swedish at noon on Christmas Eve. The text dates from 1834, because the original text from the Middle Ages was destroyed by fire. The townspeople, gathered at the steps of the city hall, join their voices in singing Martin Luther's hymn, "A Mighty Fortress Is Our God" (*Jumala ompi linnamme*). This hymn appeared in 1583, in the first Finnish psalm book. The program has been broadcast by radio to the whole nation since 1935, and today it is also broadcast on television.

Outdoor Christmas trees are very common today in city centers. They have been a feature in downtown Helsinki since the 1930s. However, in the small town of Pietarsaari, the first outdoor tree appeared in 1905. Its electric lights must have been quite a sight, because this lighting was not commonly available at that time.

All stores close early on Christmas Eve, at two or three o'clock in the afternoon, and there is no bus or streetcar traffic after six o'clock. Late afternoon vesper services are held in many churches. Also, late in the afternoon, many people visit the cemeteries and place lighted candles on the graves of family members and friends. This custom began shortly after Finland's independence in 1917. Hundreds of flickering points of light beautifully illuminate the cemeteries for hours as dusk falls.

The Christmas dinner is served between five and seven o'clock. Families gather around the decorated table. Often the Christmas gospel is read, and everyone joins in singing Martin Luther's hymn "Good News from Heaven to Earth I Bring" (*Enkeli taivaan lausui näin*) that he wrote in 1535. Now the festive meal can start.

Traditional Christmas Eve Menu

Appetizers
Glassmaster's herring, Salted salmon, Liver pate

Salad
Rosolli with red dressing

Fish
Lutefish with boiled potatoes and white sauce

Meat
The Christmas Ham

Casseroles
Sweetened potato casserole
Rutabaga casserole
Carrot casserole
Liver casserole with lingonberries

Cheese
Selection of homemade cheeses

Bread
Christmas bread

Desserts
Rice porridge, fruit soup, cookies, pound cakes, filled cake, sweets

Drinks
Glög, Kalja, milk, coffee

Chapter Six

Appetizers

This recipe looks very attractive in a wide-mouth, glass jar. It is good to prepare the dish a few days ahead of time and store it in a cool place.

Glassmaster's Herring
Lasimestarinsilli

2   salted herrings
1   carrot, peeled and sliced
½   teaspoon mustard seeds
2-3 small onions, red or white, peeled and sliced sliver
    of fresh ginger (optional)
    marinade (see page 18)

If the herring is very salty, soak it in cold water overnight. Otherwise, two hours will be enough. Prepare marinade and set aside to cool. Drain the water and cut the herring into one-inch-long pieces. Put alternating layers of onions, carrots, and the herring pieces with spices in a glass dish. Pour marinade over everything. There should be enough marinade to cover the herring and vegetables completely. Keep the dish in a cool place for 2 to 3 days to bring out the full flavor.

Marinade

1	cup water
½	cup vinegar
½	cup sugar
3-4	bay leaves
3-4	whole cloves
½	tablespoon whole white peppercorns

Combine all the ingredients for the marinade and bring it to a quick boil. Lower the heat and let it simmer 5 to 10 minutes. Cool the marinade thoroughly before pouring it over the herring mixture.

Salted Salmon
Suolattu lohi

2   fresh salmon fillets (approximately 1 pound each
      or a 2-pound fillet that can be cut in half)
½   tablespoon sugar
1   tablespoon coarse salt
      sprigs of fresh dill

Check the fillets for any bones and remove them if present. Line a shallow dish with enough aluminum foil or waxed paper to fold over and cover the fish. Put some of the dill sprigs on the paper lining. Mix the sugar and salt. Sprinkle one third over the dill. Place one of the fillets, skin side down, on the dill, sugar, and salt. Sprinkle another third of the sugar-salt mixture over the fillet, and then add the other fillet skin side up. Sprinkle the remaining sugar and salt evenly over the top and add more sprigs of dill. Fold the wax paper up and over the top of the fish and close the edges. Place a weight on the fish, covering it evenly. Refrigerate for one to two days. Serve it sliced very thinly. Decorate with fresh dill.

Liver Pâté
Maksapasteija

1   pound ground beef or calf liver
½   pound ground sirloin
1   grated onion
2   ounces minced anchovies (optional)
¼   cup softened butter
1   teaspoon sugar
1   teaspoon salt
½   teaspoon white pepper
¼   teaspoon black pepper
1   egg, lightly beaten
½   cup flour
1½   cups cream or half-and-half.
1   teaspoon marjoram
½   teaspoon ginger

Combine the ground liver, ground sirloin, soft butter, anchovies, egg, onion, sugar, salt, and spices. Mix the flour and cream until well blended and stir this into the liver mixture.

Grease well a 5-by-9-inch loaf pan and pour the mixture into it. Do not fill the pan to the top to avoid cooking over. Cover the pan with foil and place it in a larger container of water. Bake at 350° F for 1½ hours. Let it cool in the water bath. When cool, remove the cover and turn the loaf onto a serving platter. Garnish with thin strips of orange peel. Liver pâté can be frozen.

Note: If you prefer grinding the liver yourself, cook it first in milk for five to seven minutes, cool, and then grind it in a

Chapter Seven

Salads

Salads begin the traditional Christmas meal. In modern times, these can be simple lettuce salads or contain some of the summer vegetables so readily available in the supermarkets today. In traditional times, however, fresh vegetables were not typically available. Some might have saved green tomatoes to ripen slowly wrapped in newpaper, but fresh lettuce was not usually part of Christmas salads. Instead, relying on what they had, the salad course was made up of vegetables that could be stored in the root cellar. Potatoes, carrots, onions, apples, and beets all could be stored through much of the winter, and could be used effectively during the Christmas season. Other foods, such as pickled beets, pickles, and herring had been put up in jars during the harvest and could be added to the salad.

Herring Salad
Rosolli tai Sillisalaatti

5-6 small potatoes
6   carrots
1   can pickled beets or 5 fresh small beets
1   small diced onion, white or red
1-2 apples, peeled and diced
2   dill pickles, diced
1   small jar (about 6 ounces) of marinated herring bits
¼   teaspoon white pepper, if desired
1-2 hard boiled eggs, chopped (optional, for decoration)

Boil the potatoes and the carrots, without peeling, in salted water. If fresh beets are used, they should be boiled separately. Do not cut the roots of the beets because the color will run, and the beets will turn brown. Reserve the water used to boil the beets. Cool the vegetables and peel them. If the vegetables are cooked a day ahead, they should be refrigerated in brown paper or newspaper so that they will stay moist. Cube the peeled potatoes, carrots, and fresh or pickled beets, but keep them in separate containers until it is time to mix and serve the salad.

Before mixing the salad, set aside a small portion of the carrots, potatoes, beets, and pickles as decoration. Combine the rest of the cooked vegetables with the diced onion, diced apples, and diced pickles. Add the white pepper and herring bits now, if desired, although the herring can also be served separately. Decorate the top of the salad with the reserved vegetables and the chopped egg. These can be arranged in stripes across the top of the salad. Serve with Dressing for Herring Salad (page 23).

Dressing for the Herring Salad

1   cup whipping cream
1-2   teaspoons vinegar (or to taste)
2-3   teaspoons water reserved from cooking the beets (or
      pickled beet juice) for color
      salt and sugar to taste

Whip the cream, but not too stiffly. Add the beet juice. When mixed, this gives the dressing a pink color. Add the vinegar, salt, and sugar. Keep both the salad and dressing chilled sep-arately until ready to serve. The dressing tops individual serv-ings of the salad.

Note: Alternatively, sour cream can be used as a dressing.

Chapter Eight

Fish

At first the Finns inhabited the coastal areas of the country, and then they moved gradually through the waterways to settle on the shores of lakes. For centuries, because of this easy access to water, it has been natural for Finns to gain their livelihood from fishing. Before refrigeration was available, most of the catch had to be dried or salted for long-term storage. However, whenever possible, fresh fish were, and still are, preferred. This made fishing a year-round activity, with ice fishing as important economically in the winter as fishing was in the summer.

A variety of fish abound in the Finnish waters, including salmon, burbot, perch, whitefish, pike, and flounder. The Baltic herring (*silakka*) is the most important ocean variety harvested. When the nets and fishing techniques were developed to produce a large-scale fishing industry, environmentalists and conservationists feared that the Gulf of Finland would be depleted of its fish populations in a few years. Luckily, it hasn't happened, and the Finns, who love fish, have a great variety available to them. In more recent years, Finns have also developed a fish-farming industry. Today, for example, wild salmon from the rivers are not served as often at the dinner table as are the rainbow trout reared and harvested from the fish farms.

The Baltic herring, still a favorite, is a modest looking fish. It is small, with a special taste, and easy to clean. It closely resembles smelt in appearance and taste. There is an old folk saying that girls who lived on the coastal areas should know close to a hundred ways to prepare a delicious dish from Baltic herring before they were married. No wonder that there were some old maids left in the villages!

The author remembers visits as a child to the Baltic Herring Fish Market (*Silakka Markkinat*). This traditional fish market has been in existence for a long time, going back many generations. It is held every October for two to three days in the Helsinki Harbor. Although one can always buy fish, this market is very special. The fishermen come in their boats from the outermost islands to sell their catch. Besides fresh fish and smoked, salted and marinated fish, there is also an unusually fine selection of vegetables, wild berries, and handicrafts available.

The Baltic herring is preserved in layers in a marinade that is a combination of bay leaves, sugar, salt, and spices. Often, the blend of a variety of spices is a carefully guarded secret, although one can buy a standard mixture from the pharmacist. The fish are stored and sold in beautiful, handmade wooden barrels. Several centuries ago, the use of salt, sugar, and mustard became common for marinating herring and other fish. Vinegar was added as well to give a special sweet and sour taste.

Fish have historically been staple to the Finnish diet, and several of dishes featuring fish are often served as appetizers during the holiday season.

The custom of eating lutefish (*Lipeäkala*) at the Christmas Eve meal is a remnant of the Catholic Church's fasting instructions that prohibited eating meat on the eve of a holy day. At one time, lutefisk was a very ordinary winter food in Scandinavian countries. When Lutheranism became the religion of Finland at the time of the Reformation, people no longer had to observe the prohibition of meat and were allowed to eat it anytime. Lutefisk, however, retained its place in the Christmas tradition and was kept as one course of the meal. Even today, lutefisk remains part of the Christmas meal, although many now serve it on *Tapaninpäivä*, the second Christmas day. Freshly salted salmon has become more popular as the fish selection at the Christmas Eve table.

In earlier times, one bought a dried codfish fillet, which was as hard as a board and needed to be soaked for many days in a strong solution of raw soda and ashes mixed with water. This process is now done commercially, and it is possible to buy lutefisk ready to cook, often vacuum packed with cooking or baking instructions on the package. Lutefisk used to be boiled in water on the top of the stove. Now, baking it in a casserole dish in the oven is often preferred since the fish breaks up so easily in boiling water unless the cooking time is controlled very carefully. Lutefisk is typically served with white sauce, boiled peeled potatoes, and green peas.

Boiled Lutefisk
Lipeäkala keitetty

2   pounds lutefisk, ready for cooking
2   quarts water
2   tablespoons salt (or less, if desired)

Cut the fish into pieces, if necessary, and tie them in cheese-cloth. Add the two quarts of water to a large saucepan. Put the fish, wrapped in the cheesecloth, into the water and cook about 10 minutes. Do not overcook. Serve with white sauce.

Note: Do not cook the lutefisk in an aluminum saucepan or the pan will discolor.

Baked Lutefisk
Lipeäkala uunissa paistettu

2   pounds lutefisk, ready for cooking
½   tablespoon salt (or to taste)

Cut the fish into pieces, if necessary. Grease a casserole dish
and lay the fish pieces in it, skin side down. Sprinkle salt on
top of the fish. Cover the dish with a lid or use aluminum foil.
Bake at 350° F for 45 minutes or more, depending on the
thickness of the pieces. Before serving, drain the liquid that
collected during baking. Serve with white sauce.

White Sauce
Valkoinen maitokastike

2   tablespoons butter
3   tablespoons flour
2½   cups whole milk
⅛   teaspoon, each, salt and white pepper, or to taste.

Melt the butter in a saucepan. Add the flour and stir well.
Add the milk gradually while stirring with a whisk. Allow the
sauce to boil gently for about 10 minutes while stirring.
Season with salt and pepper.

Chapter Nine

The Christmas Ham

For most Finnish families, the ham is the central focus of the Christmas dinner. The casseroles and salads are set around it. In the olden days, the ham was kept on the dinner table throughout the day for snacking. Perhaps the ham is a relic of the pagan times when a piglet was sacrificed to the ancient gods. It is customary to use the leftovers and the bones for a delicious pea soup. The author's mother prepared the Christmas ham in her special way.

Aino's Ham Recipe
Ainon Joulukinkku

1   6 or 7 pound fresh pork shank
     water to cover
     salt
     homemade mustard
20 whole cloves
     sugar
     breadcrumbs

To marinate the meat, cover it with salted water overnight. How much salt? The old measurement is, "add salt until a potato floats." In the morning, rinse meat and put it in a large kettle to boil for about 20 minutes. This reduces the extra salt as well as the fat content. Transfer the ham to a platter and let it cool. Then rub the whole surface with mustard. Sprinkle with sugar and breadcrumbs to cover. Insert whole cloves all over the surface. Insert a meat thermometer. Bake until internal temperature reaches 170 F. The ham should be cooked the day before it will be eaten so that it can be served cold with stewed prunes.

A very good result, with much less work involved, is obtained by choosing a precooked ham that is ready for baking. Hams are usually available from 10 to 14 pounds, but they can be cut smaller. Follow the above directions with mustard, sugar, breadcrumbs, and cloves. Bake until the internal temperature reaches 170 F. Transfer the ham to a serving platter and let it cool. This ham should also be cooked a day before it will be served.

Traditionally, the bone protruding from the end of either ham is covered with a paper decoration made of red or white tissue.

Christmas Mustard
Joulusinappi

Recipe 1

1	cup dry mustard (Colman's dry English mustard preferred)
½	cup sugar
1	cup whipping cream
2	eggs lightly beaten
2	tablespoons of vinegar or cognac
¼	teaspoon salt

Mix mustard and sugar in a saucepan. Add the cream and lightly beaten eggs. Bring to a boil, stirring continuously to avoid burning. Turn off the heat but continue stirring as the mixture starts to cool. Add the salt and the vinegar or cognac. Store in the refrigerator.

Note: The taste will improve if the mustard is allowed to stand for a few days.

Christmas Mustard
Joulusinappi

Recipe 2

1   cup dry mustard (Colman's English mustard preferred)
¾   cup sugar
1   tablespoon potato or corn starch
1   egg
1   cup cream
     liquid from a jar of dill pickles or apple sauce to thin the mustard

Mix all the ingredients except the dill pickle liquid or apple sauce in a saucepan. Bring to a boil for a few minutes, while stirring with a whisk, until the mixture starts to thicken. Remove from the heat. Let the mustard cool. Add the dill pickle liquid or the apple sauce until the mustard has the desired consistency. The apple sauce adds an interesting flavor that goes well with the ham.

[Color Plate 1] Christmas Eve dinner is laid out on a red-and-gold Marimekko tablecloth. Christmas bread, fresh fruit, and ham with mustard head the table, with rutabaga and potato casseroles, lingon berries, and *rosolli* with cream dressing displayed around them. In front are glassmaster's herring in marinade in the glass bowl, salted salmon served with dill and kiwi fruit, small rice-and-shrimp-filled pastries decorated with fresh cucumber and red pepper slices, along with cheeses and fruit.

[Color Plate 2] The Christmas coffee table is set with a red damask tablecloth. Christmas sweet bread with a selection of cookies (left), light colored Finnish fruitcake, a buttermilk cake, small saffron breads (right) in various shapes, homemade Kola candies with tissue paper, and Finnish cookies.

[Color Plate 3] The dessert table has a selection of fruit along with traditional Finnish treats. Rice porridge with an almond, mixed fruit soup (with cinnamon sugar ready for garnish), prune cream with whipped cream clouds, cranberry parfait decorated with whipped cream and grapes, as well as a selection of cookies, which includes cinnamon "S" cookies (left), Christmas ginger cookies (top), butter rings (right), and round almond balls (bottom).

[Color Plate 4] Top: The glög table is set with a handwoven Finnish straw runner. The Christmas prune tarts have a light dusting of powdered sugar to give them the appearance of snowflakes. Bottom: The antique cheese mold and handwoven linen tablecloth set the background for home-made cheeses and pastries. Karelian pastries (left) with butter and egg spread compiment the but-termilk cheese decorated with red peppers. The flat cheese with herbs has the indentation from the cheese mold. Small pastries with onion and mushroom filling (right) and grill flat cheese decorated with grapes completes the table.

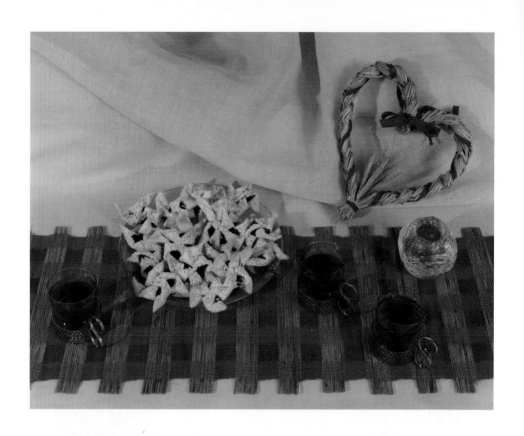

Chapter Ten

Casseroles

Rutabaga was known and harvested in some areas of the southern parts of the country since the Middle Ages. The white-fleshed turnip is probably the oldest of the cool- season crops grown in Finland. It is easily prepared for a snack, and it is a good addition to a salad when peeled and finely shredded. However, turnip typically is not used in the traditional Christmas casserole dish. It was replaced by another vegetable of the same family. The Swede-turnip, also known as rutabaga, has a firm, yellowish flesh. This vegetable found its way to the most festive dinner tables in Finland, although perhaps it was not served in the same manner as it is today, flavored with spices and sugar or syrup. It lends itself to preparation in all the traditional ways used for root vegetables. Today, rutabaga casseroles, as well as those made from potatoes and carrots, can be bought, commercially prepared, year round at any supermarket in Finland. At home, these casseroles can be prepared well ahead of the holidays and stored in the freezer. What an interesting and tasty result, and what a wonderful smell lingers in the house while the casseroles bake in the oven! The secret of the flavor of the following casseroles is in the long cooking time.

Rutabaga Casserole
Lanttulaatikko

1   large rutabaga, peeled and cut into pieces.
2   large potatoes, peeled and cut into pieces
     enough water, with about a teaspoon of salt, for boiling these vegetables.
1½ tablespoons Lyle's Golden Syrup or any light syrup
½   teaspoon nutmeg
¼   teaspoon white pepper
¼   teaspoon ginger
1½ cups of cream or whole milk
²/₃ cup of breadcrumbs
1   egg, lightly beaten.
2   tablespoons butter
     dash of salt.

Boil the vegetables in the salted water until they are soft. Drain, saving some of the liquid. Mash the vegetables together. Add the dash of salt, the syrup, the white pepper, and the spices to the rutabag-potato mixture. Retaining a small portion of dry breadcrumbs for topping the casserole, soak the rest of the crumbs in the cream or milk. Add the soaked breadcrumbs and the egg to the rutabaga-potato mixture. Add some of the cooking water, if needed, to make a slightly loose-textured mixture. Blend together well. Check the taste. Add more salt or spices, if needed.

Grease a deep casserole dish with butter and pour in the mixture. Sprinkle with retained dry breadcrumbs and dot the top with butter. Bake at about 325° F for 1½ hours or until the crust is lightly browned.

Potato Casseroles

For centuries white potatoes have been a staple ingredient in meal planning the year round. They were boiled, used in porridge, and used for baking in pasties and bread. In most of Finland, potatoes gradually replaced turnips as a basic vegetable. From the western part of the country, the sweetened potato casserole is among the favorites served at the festive table. It is an easy dish to prepare. In this recipe, flour is used as the sweetener in the potato mixture. Also, for the best results, this mix should stand five or six hours at room temperature, or, if time allows, overnight. Use a deep casserole dish. The mixture bubbles and will spill over if the dish is too shallow.

Sweetened Potato Casserole
Imelletetty perunalaatikko

2½   pounds peeled potatoes (about 8 or 9 large potatoes)
4-5   tablespoons flour
3   tablespoons butter, melted
½   cup milk
1   teaspoon salt
½   tablespoon syrup, such as Lyle's Golden Syrup
    (optional)
1   tablespoon breadcrumbs
½   teaspoon nutmeg (optional)

Boil the potatoes with the skins on. Drain and peel the potatoes when they are cooked through and cooled enough to handle. Mash the potatoes, add the flour to the mix, blend and cover the bowl. Avoid over-beating the potatoes with an electric beater and do not use a food processor; either implement will change the texture of the potatoes and produce a liquid-like casserole. Keep the bowl covered in a warm place for several hours or overnight. Stir it several times.

Add milk and butter to the mixture. Add some more milk if the mixture is not smooth and somewhat loose (the consistency of the mixture will depend on the type of potatoes used). If you prefer a sweeter casserole, add ½ tablespoon of syrup. Add salt and mix well. Grease two baking dishes and fill each of them two-thirds full with the potato mixture. Do not overfill, or the casserole may boil over. You may use a fork to make decorative patterns on the surface of each casserole. Dust with breadcrumbs and a dash of nutmeg (optional). Bake at 300° F for 2½ to 3 hours until the top is lightly browned.

Note: The casserole can be prepared and frozen before baking. Allow defrosting time before baking.

Carrot Casserole

Carrots are relatively new to the Finnish table. They were harvested in some areas of the country for the past century, but they did not become popular until they were introduced through the home economics classes at the turn of the century. We must remind ourselves that Finland was very much a rural society until World War II. These home economics courses were valuable resources for informing the population about new methods for preparing foods from different parts of the country and for introducing recipes for new vegetables, fruits, and spices. It also encouraged keeping the great provincial cooking traditions alive.

The attractive, colorful carrot casserole is a delightful adornment on the festive table. There are several versions, but this one is our favorite because it includes rice that gives the casserole a lighter taste and smoother texture. It is of interest that rice was known in Finland since the Middle Ages. It could not have grown there. Anyone who imported it must have sold it to very few traders because of its high cost. For a long time rice was a special dish to be served only at the wealthiest homes at Christmastime.

Carrot Casserole
Porkkanalaatikko

⅔   cup rice
2   cups water
1½   pounds carrots, peeled and grated
½   cup light cream
⅛   teaspoon salt
½   tablespoon sugar
⅛   teaspoon nutmeg
½   teaspoon cinnamon
1   egg, beaten
2   tablespoons butter
1   tablespoon breadcrumbs
   dash ground white pepper

Cook the rice until it is fluffy and soft and the water has been absorbed. Do not let it scorch or burn. Add some light cream if more liquid is needed. Stir occasionally. Add the raw carrots, salt, white pepper, the spices, and the egg to the cooked rice. Mix well. Grease a casserole dish with butter and pour in the mixture. Sprinkle with breadcrumbs and dot with butter. Bake at 350° F for 1½ hours, or until the top is lightly brown.

Note: You can cook the carrots first and mash them. This will give the dish a much softer texture than you will get using grated raw carrots.

Liver Casserole
Maksalaatikko

1	cup rice
2½	cups water
2	teaspoons salt
2	small onions, peeled and chopped
2	tablespoons butter for the onions
1	teaspoon white pepper
1	teaspoon marjoram
1	teaspoon ginger
4	tablespoons syrup
1	cup raisins
1	egg, beaten lightly
2	cups cream
1	pound ground liver, fresh or cooked

Boil the rice until all the water is absorbed. Simmer the onions in the butter until they are clear. Mix the onions, the rice, syrup, raisins, and spices with the ground liver. Mix the cream and egg and pour it into the casserole mixture. Mix the ingredients well. The texture will be quite loose if the liver is freshly ground in a commercial meat grinder at the butcher's. During the baking, the raisins and the rice will absorb more of the liquid. You may dot the top of casserole with butter. Bake it at 350° F for about 1½ hours or until set and lightly browned. If you use cooked liver, the baking time will be shorter, about 30 to 40 minutes. Cranberry or lingonberry jam is the delicious and traditional accompaniment for the casserole.

Chapter Eleven

Cheese

Dairy products have always played an important role in the diet of the Finnish people. In the olden days, the adults did not normally drink milk. Instead, they drank products derived from milk, such as buttermilk, of which there were two kinds. Today, the large selection of available dairy products, including milk, sour milk, butter, and cheeses, will certainly satisfy the most demanding consumer. *Viili*, probably the most popular milk product, is produced by bacterial cultures acting on milk. It resembles yogurt but is much smoother in texture and has no bitter side taste.

From milk also come the cheeses that have been made in Finnish farm kitchens for centuries. Over thirty different kinds of cheese are produced in Finland today. The following two cheese recipes are popular at Christmas and are easy to make.

Egg Cheese or Buttermilk Cheese
Munajuusto tai Piimäjuusto

3	quarts milk
1	quart buttermilk
3	eggs
1	teaspoon salt (or to taste)

Boil the milk in a kettle with a heavy bottom. Keep stirring continuously to keep the milk from sticking to the bottom of the pan. Whip together buttermilk and the eggs and add this mixture to the hot milk. Stir well. Bring the mixture back to the boiling point to separate the cheese curds. Take the kettle off the heat and keep at room temperature until the mixture curdles completely.

Line a sieve with a damp cheesecloth and transfer the cheese curds into it using a slotted spoon. Some water will drain out immediately. Add the salt and mix with a spoon. Fold the edges of the cheesecloth over the top of the cheese. (Use a Finnish handmade wooden cheese mold, if available. Its carved design makes beautiful, decorative cheese when unmolded.) Put some weight on the cheese. Let it drain several hours or overnight, in the refrigerator. Invert the cheese onto a serving dish.

This cheese can be baked. Traditionally, it was laid on some straw and baked quickly in a very hot oven so that the cheese developed a beautiful, golden brown crust. Add spices to the cheese such as garlic and different kinds of herbs, if desired.

Cheese and antique mold.

This very mild cheese was one of the author's favorite presents during her childhood when her relatives came to visit from Pohjanmaa, a province in the western part of Finland. She liked the squeaky sound one hears when biting into the cheese. It is often served plain but it can also be served with jam.

Homemade Flat Cheese
Juoksetejuusto

4   quarts milk
1   teaspoon salt
3   rennet tablets (These are available from
    a pharmacist.)
2   tablespoons water

Heat the milk to lukewarm. Crush the rennet tablets. Add water and stir until the tablets are totally dissolved. Pour the water mixture and salt into the warm milk. Leave the milk in a warm place for about four hours, covered with a cloth. During this time, the mixture will begin to form curds; it should not be stirred or touched throughout the entire cheese-making process. Line a sieve with damp cheesecloth, and with a slotted spoon, lift the cheese mass into it. Allow the cheese to drain overnight in a cool place. Do not forget to put a deep dish under the sieve to collect the dripping whey. When the cheese is fairly dry, bring the corners of the cheesecloth together and mold it into a flat square or press it into a round form. Invert it onto a cake pan with high edges and let the cheese set. Discard any whey. Put the cheese under a broiler for 3 to 4 minutes or until the surface is lightly browned in patches. Do not let it burn. Turn it over and put it again under the broiler. Small amounts of whey will still be running out of the cheese. Sprinkle it with salt and let it cool thoroughly before serving.

Chapter Twelve

Christmas Breads

Bread making has had great importance for Christmas preparations, but it was also part of basic nutrition. For centuries the farmers have sown various grains, including rye, barley, wheat, and oats. In the past, bad weather conditions such as a late frost could prevent farmers from plowing and sowing, or heavy rains in the fall could easily ruin most of the grain harvest. The "hunger years" (*Nälkä vuodet*), between 1695 and 1697, were a terrible time when a third of population died of starvation. Again in 1867 and 1868 a great part of the population had to add ground bark or lichen to their flour to stretch it to make bread.

Finland has an interesting history of breadmaking because of the combination of food traditions from the eastern part of the country, influenced by Russian baking, mixed with those of the coastal regions in the West and South. This combination produced an unusual result, in that breads in everyday use in the eastern part of the country could be served as a specialty in the coastal areas on festive occasions. Today the regional breads are available across the country and eaten as everyday breads.

When the first baking was done with the freshly milled flour, the bread had a symbolic meaning. The loaf was large and decorated with straw. This was called the Show Bread. It was brought to the table at Christmas, and other breads were piled around it. This bread was not eaten but put away in the cellar and covered with straw until spring when it was either eaten or crumbled and spread on the fields as a blessing for the new growing season. In some farm households, it was customary to bake only twice a year. The rye bread was baked with the hole in the middle, dried to prevent spoilage and threaded on a long beam that was often the length of the country kitchen (*tupa*).

This bread has kept its popularity as a special Christmas bread because Finns don't sweeten everyday breads. The lightly browned crust and the sweet aroma of orange peel, fennel, and anise make this very special.

Christmas Bread
Joululimppu

4	cups buttermilk
3	ounces fresh yeast or 2 packages of dry yeast
¾	cup dark syrup
2	teaspoons ground fennel seeds
2	teaspoons anise
2	teaspoons grated fresh orange peel
2	teaspoons salt
3	cups rye flour (approximately)
1½	cups graham flour
4	cups flour
2	teaspoons caraway seeds (optional)

Liquid for brushing loaves

½	cup water
1	tablespoon syrup

Heat the buttermilk to lukewarm. Crumble in the fresh yeast and add the syrup and spices. If using dry yeast, follow the package directions. Mix in the flour and knead thoroughly. Cover the dough with a cloth and put it in a warm place to rise, or put the covered bowl in warm water to rise. Divide the dough into two or three parts, depending on the desired size of the finished loaves. Shape the portions into round loaves and place them on a greased cookie sheet. Let them rise in a warm place. Prick them with a fork before placing them in the oven. Bake about 30 to 35 minutes at 400° F. When the breads are still warm, brush with the syrup water mixture. Decorate with caraway seeds, if desired.

Pulla

This sweetbread or *pulla*, as it is often called in Finnish, is a
crown for any festivity as well as a wonderful slice of bread any time
with coffee or tea. At Christmas time, the dough is formed into
gingerbread men for the children. Raisins are the eyes, and their
coats have raisin buttons. A light brushing of egg before baking
gives them a shine when they come from the oven. There are several ways to create fancy sweetbreads, but perhaps the most popular form for a large gathering is a circle. Customarily, the center is
filled with freshly baked cookies. The cardamom spice gives the
sweetbread a special taste. If they are available, use whole car-
damoms. Peel the pods and crush the seeds to make the spice. The
crushed cardamom seeds will taste stronger than the cardamom
powder in the sweetbread.

Christmas Sweet Bread (page 52) formed into braid and other shapes.

Christmas Sweet Bread after baking.

Christmas Sweet Bread
Jouluvehnänen

2   cups milk
2   ounces fresh yeast or 2 packages dry yeast
3   eggs
1⅓ cups sugar
1½ teaspoons salt
1½ teaspoons cardamom
1   cup soft butter
8½ cups flour (approximately)

Crumble the fresh yeast in two tablespoons of water. Let stand 10 minutes. If using dry yeast, dissolve the yeast in lukewarm water according to the package directions. Heat the milk until warm (hand temperature). Add to it the fresh or dry yeast, sugar, spices, and lightly beaten eggs. Add enough of the flour to give a thick, elastic mixture. Beat it vigorously to put air into the dough. This will make the dough rise well.

Mix in the rest of the flour and finally the soft butter. Knead the dough well. Cover it with a kitchen towel and let it rise in a warm place. When the dough has doubled in bulk (in about an hour), place it on a lightly floured surface and knead well.

Form the dough into a straight, braided loaf or make many different shapes. Let these rise about 30 minutes.

Glaze the loaves with beaten egg (one egg and one yolk), and if desired, sprinkle pearl sugar and chopped or sliced almonds on the top. Bake at 400° F for about 20 minutes or, for the smaller buns, 10 to 15 minutes. These breads can be frozen.

Chapter Thirteen

Desserts

Victoria's Dessert
Viktorian jälkiruoka

2 cups cold leftover rice porridge
1 cup whipping cream
2 tablespoons sugar
1 teaspoon vanilla or one tablespoon vanilla sugar
2 tablespoons lemon juice
1 envelope gelatin plus two tablespoons cold water

Whip the cream. Add the cream, sugar, vanilla, and lemon juice to the cold porridge. Soften gelatin in the cold water and place it over hot water until dissolved. Fold gelatin into the rice and whipping cream mixture. Decorate with fresh or frozen berries.

Prune Pudding
Luumukiisseli

1   eight-ounce package pitted prunes
3   cups water
1   cinnamon stick
2   tablespoons sugar
2   tablespoons potato starch and half a cup of water
    lemon juice to taste

Put the prunes and the water in a saucepan. Add the cinnamon stick and the sugar and bring to a boil. Cover and simmer 15 to 20 minutes. Transfer the prunes into a dessert bowl. Save the liquid. Remove the cinnamon stick. Mix the potato starch and cold water to make a smooth paste and pour it slowly into the liquid while stirring. Simmer until it thickens and becomes transparent. Season with lemon juice. Pour over the prunes. Sprinkle with sugar to prevent a crust from forming. Cool. This dessert should be served with whipped cream.

Prune Cream
Luumukermahyytelö

1   eight-ounce package pitted prunes
1¼ cups water
1   envelope Knox gelatin and 2 tablespoons cold water
2   cups whipping cream
¼   cup sugar

Cook the prunes in a covered saucepan 15 to 20 minutes. Cool. Purée the stewed prunes with the cooking liquid in a blender or food processor. Soften the gelatin in the cold water and place it over hot water until dissolved. Whip the cream while adding the sugar to it. Stir in the dissolved gelatin. Fold in the puréed prunes. Pour into a dessert dish or mold. Chill the dessert for a few hours before serving.

Cranberry Parfait
Karpalovaahto

2   cups cranberry juice made from fresh cranberries
or frozen cranberry juice
1   envelope Knox gelatin and 2 tablespoons cold water
½   cup sugar or to taste

Bring the cranberry juice and sugar to a boil in a saucepan. Soften the gelatin in the cold water and add it to the hot juice. Keep the saucepan over low heat, stirring constantly until the gelatin is dissolved. Remove from heat and chill until slightly thicker than the consistency of unbeaten egg white. Beat with an electric beater until light and fluffy and double in volume. Spoon into a dessert bowl or individual dishes. Chill until firm.

1 cup whipped cream can be folded into the parfait. However, if this option is desired, use only 1½ cups of cranberry juice instead of 2 cups.

Chapter Fourteen

With Dinner Over

With dinner over, the time of greatest excitement for children is at hand. Father Christmas will soon arrive with his presents. The Finnish word for Father Christmas is *Joulupukki*, which literally means Christmas goat. Very likely, this name is an indication that he was once associated with an animal figure, namely the straw goat of the harvest festivals. The straw goat took on a human form but retained the animal name. Today, *Joulupukki* is dressed in a red outfit. He looks quite different than he did in earlier times when his gray lamb coat was worn inside out, and his stern mask made him look very somber. He often comes in person to deliver the gifts, or he may just knock at the door and leave the gifts in a gunny sack or a bark basket in the entrance hall. *Joulupukki* starts his trip from *"Korvatunturi"* an imaginary mountain in Lapland. This mountain is located close to the Russian border. His home was established there in 1927 by Uncle Marcus (*Markus-setä*), a radio personality who produced a wonderful one-hour program for children every Saturday evening from the Finnish Broadcasting Company in Helsinki.

What does the name *Korvatunturi* mean? *Korva* means "ear" and *tunturi* means "mountain." There are no roads to take you there. It remains a mystical place for *Joulupukki* and his little elf helpers, *tontut*. However, he has established a post office service in Rovaniemi, Lapland, where he answers letters from children all around the world. His sleigh, pulled by only one reindeer, resembles those used by the Lapps, and during Christmas Eve he miraculously manages to visit all the Finnish children! After all the activity of receiving and opening gifts, everybody is ready for coffee, cookies, cakes, and tarts.

In earlier times in Germany, an angel was thought to bring Christmas presents to children. They could hear silver bells ringing when presents were placed under the tree, but they never caught a glimpse of the gift-giver. Christmas angels in Finland are likely to be viewed as guardian angels and are featured in Christmas decorations and children's plays. *Joulupukki* has always delivered the gifts.

Chapter Fifteen

Christmas Cookies

In the 1920s, cookie recipes, previously carefully guarded by cooks and bakers, became widely available through magazines and home economics classes. A new assortment of baked goods appeared at all kinds of celebrations, not only at Christmas.

The history of ginger cookies goes back to the Middle Ages. These ginger cookies were not the thin variety, sweetened with syrup and ginger, that we associate with Christmas today. They contained a good dose of pepper and were often baked in the form of small balls instead of cookie-cutter shapes. In fact, two centuries ago, the Swedish naturalist, Linne, recommended ginger cookies as a preventive medicine, especially for stomach illnesses. The following recipe is our favorite. One can vary the taste by adjusting the relative amounts of the spices. The dough can be frozen and baked when more cookies are needed.

Christmas Ginger Cookies
Joulupiparkakut

10	ounces butter or margarine
1¼	cups sugar
3	eggs
1	cup dark syrup
2	teaspoons cinnamon
2	teaspoons ginger
2	teaspoons cloves (powdered or crushed very fine)
1	tablespoon grated orange rind
½	teaspoon cardamom (optional)
7	cups flour (approximately)
3	teaspoons baking soda

Boil the syrup and spices. Add to the butter or margarine and stir until the mixture is cool. Beat the eggs and sugar together. Mix the soda in with part of the flour and then combine with the syrup-margarine mixture. Add the whipped eggs and the rest of the flour. Cover the dough and leave overnight in the refrigerator.

Dust a baking board with flour, and roll out the dough. Cut it into different shapes using a variety of cookie cutters. Bake at 400° F about 10 minutes until golden brown.

Christmas Ginger Cookies (page 54). Rolled out dough cut with cutters.

Ginger Cookies, baked and decorated

61

Cinnamon "S" Cookies
Kaneli ässät

1	cup (minus 1 tablespoon) butter or margarine
¾	cup sugar
2	eggs
2	teaspoons baking powder
2¼	cups white flour
	mixture of 3 teaspoons cinnamon and
	3 tablespoons sugar

Beat the butter and sugar until fluffy. Add the eggs one at a time beating well. Mix the baking powder and the flour and fold into the mixture. Let the dough rest in the refrigerator for a couple of hours.

Shape the dough into four-inch-long sticks the thickness of a little finger. Roll them in the sugar and cinnamon mixture and form into "S" shapes on the cookie sheet. Bake at 340° F for 10 to 12 minutes until golden brown.

Karin's Butter Rings
Karinin voirinkilät

4½ ounces butter
4   tablespoons heavy cream
2   cups flour
½   teaspoon vanilla extract
    pearl sugar for decoration
    water or egg white

Stir butter until soft and white. Add cream, vanilla, and flour. Mix well and set in a cool place for half an hour. Dust the baking surface with flour. Roll the dough to such a length that the thickness is about the same as a little finger. Cut it to five-inch lengths. Brush the top of each piece with water or egg white. Pour some pearl sugar in a shallow dish. Dip the pieces in the sugar with the moistened side down. Lay each one on a baking sheet, sugar side up, and make a ring form. Bake at 350° F about 10 minutes, or until the top is golden in color. Let the cookies cool. Remove them from the baking sheet with care. These cookies will keep their texture and flavor best if stored in a cool dry place.

Almond Balls
Mantelipallot

4½   ounces butter at room temperature
1   egg
½   cup sugar
½   teaspoon vanilla extract
½   tablespoon grated orange rind
½   tablespoon grated lemon rind
½   tablespoon lemon juice
1   cup flour (Add more if needed to form the
      dough into balls.)
½   cup ground almonds
      finely chopped almonds for coating the balls

Separate the egg white and yolk. Mix together egg yolk, butter, sugar, almonds, and spices. Then add the flour to made a dough. Form the dough into small balls. Dip these first in egg white then roll them in finely chopped almonds. You can add a red cherry on the top, if you wish. Bake at 400° F until light brown.

Cookies for the Gentry
Herrasväen leivät

8   ounces, less 1 tablespoon, butter
½   cup sugar
⅔   cup potato starch flour
1⅓   cup flour
     raspberry or some other jam
     sugar for decoration.

Beat the softened butter and sugar until foamy. Mix both flours together and add this to the butter-sugar mixture. Work until it is well blended. Chill in the refrigerator.

On the floured board, roll out the dough quite thin and cut it into rounds about two inches in diameter using a cutter. Place the cookies on a greased baking sheet and bake in a 400° F oven for 10 to 15 minutes.

Let the cookies cool thoroughly. Take two cookies and spread jam between them. For a decorative effect, press both sides of the cookies in sugar.

Hazelnut Cookies
Pähkinäpyörykät

2   eggs
1   cup sugar
7   ounces ground hazelnuts
    whole hazelnuts for decoration

Beat the eggs and sugar until light and fluffy. Fold in the ground hazelnuts. Take a rounded teaspoon of the batter and drop it on a very well-greased cookie sheet (preferably lined with parchment paper) well apart from each other. Drop one hazelnut on the top of each cookie. Bake at 325° F for 15 to 20 minutes.

Chapter Sixteen

Christmas Cakes and Tarts

This recipe is from the author's aunt, age eighty-six, who operated a catering service in Somero, Finland. She still bakes fabulous cakes for parties using a wood-burning stove.

Aunt Aura's Lemon Cake
Aura tädin sitruuna kakku

¾   cup butter
1½   cups sugar
5   eggs
3   ounces raisins
⅓   cup cream
3   cups flour
2   teaspoons baking powder
1   tablespoon fresh lemon rind
¼   cup freshly squeezed lemon juice

Cream the sugar and butter. Add the eggs, one at a time, beating them well into the sugar and butter mixture. Add the lemon juice and rind. Mix flour and baking powder and add it gradually, alternating with the cream, to the eggs and butter mixture. Add the raisins.

Grease a cake pan and dust it lightly with breadcrumbs. Pour in the cake mixture. Bake at 325° F for about an hour or test with a toothpick until it comes out dry.

Buttermilk Cake
Piimäkakku

$1\frac{1}{3}$ cup buttermilk
2   teaspoons baking soda
$\frac{1}{2}$ cup brown sugar
7   ounces butter, melted
1   cup raisins or chopped dried apricots
2   tablespoons cognac (optional)
$\frac{1}{2}$ cup Lyle's golden syrup

Sift the following dry ingredients together:

$2\frac{1}{2}$ cups white flour
2   tablespoons cocoa powder
1   teaspoon cinnamon
$\frac{1}{2}$ teaspoon ginger
$\frac{1}{2}$ teaspoon cloves
$\frac{1}{2}$ teaspoon ground cardamom
$\frac{1}{2}$ teaspoon grated orange peel

Mix the buttermilk and the soda. Add the sugar, butter, syrup, cognac (if desired), and dried fruit followed by the dry ingredients. Mix quickly. Pour the batter into a well-buttered, floured tube pan and bake at 350° F for 50 minutes. Cool in the pan.

For this cake one may use a variety of ground nuts, but the hazelnuts have a distinct flavor that is well suited to this cake.

Hazelnut Cake
Hasselpähkinä kakku

3   eggs
1⅓   cups sugar
1⅓   cups flour
1½   cups ground hazelnuts
2   teaspoons baking powder
10½ tablespoons melted butter
⅔   cup milk

Beat the eggs and sugar until fluffy and thick. Mix the ground nuts and baking powder into the flour and fold these carefully with the melted butter and milk into the beaten eggs and sugar.

Pour the batter into a very well-buttered and floured tube pan. Bake at 350° F for about one hour. Let it cool before removing from the pan.

Spice Cake
Maustekakku

5½ tablespoons butter
½   cup plus 2 tablespoons dark corn syrup
½   cup sugar
1   teaspoon ginger
1   teaspoon ground cardamom
2   teaspoons cinnamon
1   teaspoon grated orange peel
½   teaspoon cloves
3   eggs
1½ cups flour
2   teaspoons baking powder
½   cup raisins

Bring the butter, syrup, sugar, and spices to a boil. Allow this to cool. Add the eggs one at a time. Beat well. Mix the baking powder, flour, and raisins. Fold them into the batter. Bake in a well-buttered tube cake pan at 350° F for about one hour.

This cake keeps well for a long time even without freezing. Before serving, dust the cake with powdered sugar to give it a festive appearance.

Finnish Fruitcake
Suomalainen hedelmäkakku

5½ ounces butter
1   cup sugar
3   eggs
6   ounces chopped mixed dried fruits and raisins
½   cup chopped almonds
2   tablespoons lemon juice or rum
1   cup plus 1 tablespoon white flour
½   cup potato starch flour or corn starch
2   teaspoons baking powder
1   teaspoon vanilla
1   teaspoon ground cardamom

Cream the butter with the sugar until light and fluffy. Add the eggs, one by one, beating until the mixture is very light and thick. Sift the flour and baking powder and sprinkle two tablespoons of this mixture over the dried fruits and almonds, tossing them to coat well. This step is important to prevent the fruits and almonds from accumulating at the bottom of the cake. Sift the remaining flour into the creamed mixture and blend until the batter is smooth. Fold in the fruits and almonds and the lemon juice or rum. Turn the batter into a well-buttered tube cake pan or loaf pan. Bake at 350° F for about one hour.

As with all fruitcakes, the flavor of this cake will improve with aging. Wrap the cake and store it a few days before serving.

Christmas Tarts (page 73), showing how to fold the dough over the filling.

These traditional prune-filled Christmas tarts are typically shaped into two different forms. It is not unusual to hear family members and friends discussing their choice between a star or a moon, but both shapes taste very good. Here are two equally delicious pastry recipes to try. The filling and baking methods are the same for both. These tasty and popular tarts are found in every bakery and café at Christmas time in Finland and are easy and fun to make at home.

Christmas Tarts
Joulutortut

Pastry 1

8	ounces butter or margarine
2½	cups flour
8	ounces small curd cottage cheese
1½	teaspoons baking powder (optional)
	powdered sugar for decorating

Mix the butter, flour, and baking powder. Stir in the cottage cheese and form into a ball. Do not overwork the dough. Flour the baking board and roll out the dough.

Pastry 2

2	cups flour
⅔	cup water
2	tablespoons vinegar
7	ounces butter, softened

Mix the flour, water, and vinegar. Add the butter and form the dough into a ball. Do not overwork the dough. Flour the baking board and roll out the dough.

Filling

1	pound pitted prunes
1½	cups water for stewing prunes
½	cup sugar
1	tablespoon lemon juice
	dash of cinnamon

Cut the pastry dough into 3-inch squares using a small pizza cut-ter. To form the star, make a cut from each corner of a square halfway to the center. Simmer the prunes in one and one-half cups water until soft. Mash the prunes while they are still warm and sea-son with lemon juice, sugar, and cinnamon. Put a small spoonful of the filling in the center of each square and fold alternating corners to the center to form a pinwheel star. Allow the stars to rise for 15 minutes before baking. Brush the stars with lightly beaten egg.

Bake at 400 F for about 15 minutes until the stars are gold-en brown. Do not over bake. When the stars are partly cooled, sprinkle them with powdered sugar.

Follow the above recipe to make half moon shapes. Cut round forms using a cookie cutter. Fill the center with filling and turn one half over the other and press the sides together. Brush with egg. Bake about 15 minutes at 400° F. Do not use commercial fillings. The jam will leak out of the tarts during baking due to the high sugar content.

Chapter Seventeen

Sweets

Sweets used as gifts have a long history going back to Roman times. During festivals, sweets were given as gifts, and it has been assumed that these treats had a symbolic meaning, perhaps a wish for a long and happy life. For centuries, marzipan figurines, made of a mixture of almonds and sugar, have been especially popular gifts at Christmas time. These beautifully made pigs and other animal figures may reflect an ancient pagan custom of offering an animal at the feast time.

Sugar came into wider use after the first sugar factory in Finland was established in the eighteenth century. Homemade candies were common treats until the commercial production of confectionery and chocolate started. The oldest firm was founded about a hundred years ago by a skilled and adventurous Swiss entrepreneur named Karl Fazer. He brought along his knowledge of Konditory products and later sent his son to Paris to study the art of confectionery making. As a result, a very successful and sweet industry was born.

The following old Christmas folk song verse reflects the custom of hanging sweets on the Christmas tree as decorations:

The Christmas tree has been trimmed
Joulupuu on rakenettu
Christmas is upon us
Joulu on jo ovella
Sweets have been hung
Namusia ripustettu
On the branches of the tree.
Ompi kuusen oksilla

These sweets were made of sugar and water and resembled hard candy. They were wrapped in colored tissue paper or sparkling cellophane paper. There were decorated with beautiful stickers of flowers, birds, and angels. One can still buy these candies today although it is easy to make them oneself.

Chocolate had, and still has, a special appeal as an after-dinner sweet along with a variety of nuts and dried fruits on the Christmas Eve side table. The author's uncle, as a child, considered raisins a special treat when he wanted something very sweet.

The first taste of chocolate was truly unique for a country boy, like my father. When he was a five-year-old child, he traveled at Christmas with his own father to visit his grandparents. The ride was long. My father had tried very hard to sit properly most of the time because he was worried about having his new, well-pressed sailor's outfit wrinkled or soiled. Opposite him sat a man who turned out to be a sea captain who was very pleased to see a young child behaving so well. The gentleman, after talking with my father, got up from his seat and left to return with a trunk. This he opened and took out a large box that was decorated with pictures of castles in a foreign country. He lifted the lid of the box and the whole compartment was suddenly filled with the wonderful aroma of chocolate. Then he asked my father to select two pieces of that marvelous chocolate. It must have been a very difficult decision to make. In later years, as an adult, my father seemed to be in constant search of chocolate candy that could match the flavor of the chocolate he enjoyed as a child on the train in 1915.

This chocolate candy is known by several names, including Cream Kola Candy and French Kola Cream Candy. It resembles fudge.

Kola Candies
Kola karamellit

1½	cups sugar
2	tablespoons honey
1	cup cream
¼	cup cocoa powder
2	tablespoons butter
½	cup chopped hazelnuts or almonds
⅛	teaspoon vanilla sugar (optional)

In a heavy kettle, mix the sugar, honey, cream, vanilla, and cocoa powder and bring to a boil. Simmer 20 to 30 minutes, stirring frequently. When a drop of the mixture hardens in ice cold water, remove the pan from the heat and stir in the butter and nuts. Grease an 8-inch-by-8-inch dish. Pour in the mixture and allow the candy to cool before cutting into pieces.

Chapter Eighteen

Drinks

In the earlier times people made Christmas beer at home. Now beer is available commercially. Many families, however, still make their own Christmas *kalja*, a very popular non-alcoholic malt table drink. It is made of rye malt flour, water, and sugar, with a tiny bit of yeast added. Yeast creates a slight fermentation and gives the drink a special taste along with the taste of the malt.

Another popular Christmas drink is *glög*. It found its way from Swedish manor homes to Finland, first among the Swedish speaking population and later among all Finns, thus becoming a true Finnish Christmas tradition also. It is a favorite at parties and gatherings at work and at home.

Here are a few of the many recipes for *glög*, made with and without alcohol.

Glög with Alcohol

1	bottle red wine
½	cup sugar or to taste
	peel of one lemon, grated
	piece of a cinnamon stick
	small piece of ginger
	cloves (10 to 15)
½	cup vodka or other hard liquor

Add the spices to the wine. Heat it, but do not boil. Add hard liquor. Serve promptly.

Non-alcoholic Glög with Grape Juice

2   cups grape or apple juice
½   cup spiced liquid (see the recipe below)
     peeled almonds
     raisins

Spiced liquid for Glög

1   quart water
2   pieces of ginger
2   cinnamon sticks
     whole cloves (25 to 30)
2   tablespoons cardamom seeds, not crushed
1   cup raisins

Boil the spices in the water for about an hour. Let it cool. Strain and store in the refrigerator.

Put a few raisins and almonds in the bottom of each glass. Combine the juice and spiced liquid in a kettle and heat. Pour into glasses. Proportions of juice and spiced liquid may be adjusted.

Non-alcoholic Glög

2   cups water
     whole cloves (4 or 5)
2   cinnamon sticks
¼   teaspoon cardamom seeds, not crushed
3-4 dried figs
4   cups black currant or cranberry juice
     sugar according to taste

Boil the water and spices until the liquid evaporates to half of the original amount. Strain. Add the juice. If too strong, add more water. Heat it and serve with raisins and peeled almonds.

Chapter Nineteen

Christmas Cards

Although the first known Christmas card was sent in England in 1843, the tradition of sending greeting cards to relatives and friends is only about 100 years old in Finland. Most likely, the first cards were imported from Sweden and Germany. During the early years of Finnish independence, young patriotic artists such as Martta Wendalin began to create Christmas card designs that reflected Finnish symbols of Christmas. Popular themes included straw ornaments, birds, scenes of snow-filled woods, and children. The oldest Christmas card that has survived in Finland was sent in 1887.

One of the favorite Christmas card designs has been an arrangement of flocks of European bullfinches, *Punatulkku*. These red-breasted birds are often pictured in the barnyard landscapes sitting on sheaves of grain. It is still customary to put out these grain sheaves for the birds in the countryside. These reminders of country life may also be seen set up on balconies in cities.

Another Christmas card theme unique to Finnish culture was a picture of a young bather in the sauna. The image of a small child vigorously beating his legs with a bundle of birch leaves, or *vihta*, and the Christmas greeting on the card let the person receiving the card know that the child was enjoying a traditional Christmas sauna.

Other familiar characters on Christmas cards in Finland are the little elves called *tontut*. They are playful friends of Santa Claus and children. Nobody quite knew what they looked like until a Swedish artist, Jenny Nystrom, created a *tonttu* one hundred years ago. They are usually painted in gray or red outfits wearing pointed red woolen caps. This image of the tonttu is recognized throughout Scandinavia. He appears in Christmas activities, helps Santa Claus and makes an appearance in children's plays. Rice porridge is a favorite Christmas food of the little elves who are so much a part of Finnish Christmas stories. According to the folk tales, some of which go as far back as medieval times, the Christmas porridge had to be shared with the house elves who were believed to have lived in different places on the farm, such as in the threshing house, stable, sauna, or attic. These elves were usually kind and protected the house, especially the children. However, when they thought themselves mistreated, they could get noisy and show their displeasure in some unpleasant way toward the farm folk.

Because of the scarcity of rice, this dish was considered a special treat even among the wealthy in earlier times. Rice porridge is cooked in a milk base either on the top of the stove or slow cooked in the oven. From Sweden came a custom to hide a blanched almond in the Christmas porridge. Whoever found it in his or her rice porridge would be prosperous and successful in the coming year.

Tonttu's Rice Porridge
Tontun Riisipuuro

1½   cups water
1   cup rice (Use short grain or medium grain rice because the long grain does not stick together.)
3   cups milk
½   teaspoon salt, or to taste
1   blanched almond

It is preferable to use a double boiler, if you have one. Heat the water, add the rice, and cover. Bring this to a boil and let simmer about 20 minutes, until most of the water is absorbed. Now add the milk, bring the porridge to a boil again, turn the heat to a low setting, and partially cover the pot. Cook slowly until all the milk has been absorbed, and the porridge has become thick. You may need to add more milk, if the porridge is too thick. Season with salt. Add the blanched almond. Sprinkle with cinnamon and sugar and serve with milk or mixed fruit soup.

This soup is traditionally served with rice porridge but can be also served as a dessert by itself with whipped cream. In the past, this soup was a Christmas delicacy because exotic fruits were hard to get during the winter months. Sailors often brought dried fruits home to their families during Christmas.

Mixed Fruit Soup
Sekahedelmäkeitto

1	8-ounce package dried mixed fruit (figs, apricots, prunes, pears, and apples)
4	cups water
2	tablespoons lemon juice
1	teaspoon grated lemon rind (optional)
1	cinnamon stick
1/3	cup sugar
2	tablespoons potato starch or corn starch
1/3	cup cold water

Place the mixed fruit in the water and allow it to soak for a while. Add the cinnamon stick, sugar, lemon rind, and lemon juice. Bring this to a boil. Lower the heat, cover and simmer until the fruit is very soft. Transfer the fruit with a slotted spoon to the serving dish and remove the cinnamon stick. Mix the potato starch in cold water and add the mixture to the liquid, stirring constantly. Bring quickly back to a boil until the soup is clear.

Pour this mixture over the fruit and sprinkle with a little sugar. Cover the dish to prevent a skin from forming on the top.

Chapter Twenty

Christmas Continues

On Christmas Day early church services are held at six or seven o'clock in the morning. The day is usually spent quietly at home with family. However, the second Christmas day (*Tapanin päivä*), known in England as Boxing Day, is a holiday in Finland when people get together, play games, and generally make merry. Years back, sleigh riding was a popular activity in the countryside on *Tapanin päivä*. After an afternoon outing, it is nice to serve guests a pastry. Often, that would be a *piirakka*.

These pastries are very popular all year round. Deep fried small pastries, filled with ground meat and rice, perhaps taste best right at the market place beside Helsinki harbor in December. Candles are lit, and, in the freezing temperatures, hot steaming bullion is served with the warm pastries. Pastries have different shapes and names depending on their filling, but fillings with rice and mildly spiced mushrooms are the favorites for the coffee table. The following recipe will serve six to eight people. It can also be used to make about ten smaller pastries.

Salmon Pastry
Lohipiirakka

8   ounces butter
3   cups flour
5-6 tablespoons cold water

Filling

2   cups cooked and cooled rice
¾   cup cooked salmon or shrimp
1   onion, chopped
½   cup chopped mushrooms
¾   cup cream
2   tablespoons butter
     salt and pepper to taste

Glaze

egg, lightly beaten

Cut the butter and flour together, then add the water. Do not overwork the dough. Simmer the chopped onions and mushrooms together in butter until the mushrooms have no water left. Mix the rice and fish into the onion-mushroom mix. Pour in the cream. Add salt and pepper to taste.

Divide the dough in half. Roll out each half of the dough evenly to form the shape of a large dinner plate. Place one dough round on a buttered baking sheet. Fill the dough leaving ½ inch clear around the edge. Brush the edge of the dough with egg and lay the top round over. Press the edges with a fork. Prick the pie crust with a fork. Brush with egg. Bake at 400° F for 25 to 30 minutes until golden brown. Serve with sour cream. Decorate with fresh dill.

Small, rye pastries, called Karjalan piirakka, have their origin in the kitchens of Eastern Finland. After the Second World War when the Karelians resettled in other parts of Finland, they introduced their wonderful pies to their new communities. These pies, filled with rice, carrots, rutabaga, or potatoes, are popular now at the Christmas table. The crust of this pie should be quite thin, almost translucent, but a thicker crust is easier to handle for beginners.

Karelian Pastries
Karjalanpiirakat

Crust

1	cup water
1½	teaspoons salt
1⅔	cups rye flour
⅔	cup all-purpose flour.

Filling: Rice Porridge (*see* Christmas Porridge, page 85)

Glaze

½	cup water or milk
2	ounces butter

Mix salt and flour. Add water. Knead the dough until smooth. Dust the baking surface with flour. Roll the dough to an even diameter. Divide it into 18 to 20 pieces of equal length. Shape each into a ball. With a rolling pin, flatten each ball to a thin circle about six inches in diameter. Dust each circle with some flour, stack them, and cover them with a cloth. These small flat pieces for the crust should not get dry during the baking process. Add rice porridge filling in the center of each piece and spread it toward the edges. Fold the crust over the filling, leaving the center open. Crimp the edges. Bake at 450° F for 5 to 10 minutes or until the edges are golden brown. Do not burn the crust. Brush the pies, while they are still warm, with butter and water mixture. Serve with butter and egg mixture (*munavoi*).

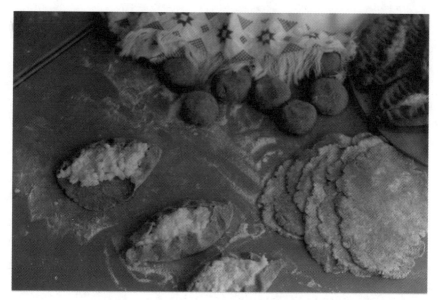

Karelian pastries (page 89), showing how to form them.

Butter and Egg Spread
Munavoi

2   hard boiled eggs, chopped
2   ounces butter
      salt and white pepper to taste

Mix these ingredients and spread over the pies.

Chapter Twenty-One

New Year's Eve

Although Finns are not especially superstitious people, they have kept alive a New Year's Eve tradition of telling fortunes from melted tin. Although in the past tin melting was mainly practiced in genteel families who had adopted this custom from Sweden, it is a popular family activity throughout Finland today. The melted shapes of tin foretell events of the coming year. A small lump of tin in the shape of a horseshoe is melted in a special ladle over a bed of hot coals in the fireplace or over a kitchen-stove element. As soon as the tin has melted, it is quickly poured into a deep bucket of cold water. This process produces a great variety of interesting shapes. Interpretation of the results can be greatly enhanced by holding these pieces in front of a light and analyzing the resulting shadows. For example, a shape resembling an airplane or boat may indicate travel in the year ahead while foam represents money. A ring could indicate an engagement in the near future. Of course, these predictions often require a great deal of imagination. Later in the evening a coffee table is set with Christmas breads and cookies, pies, open-faced sandwiches, and a filled cake.

Filled Cake
Täytekakku

4	eggs
¾	cup sugar
1	cup white flour
2	tablespoons potato or corn starch
1	teaspoon baking powder

Beat eggs and sugar together until creamy and fluffy. Mix the flour, baking powder, and potato starch together and fold carefully into the egg and sugar mixture. Grease a spring-form pan and flour well. Pour the batter into the pan and bake at 375° F for 35 to 40 minutes or until the top springs back when touched lightly. Cool and remove from the pan. Cut the cake into 2 horizontal layers. An alternate choice is to put the cake batter into two well-buttered and floured eight-inch round cake pans to make two layers.

Liquid to moisten the cake

½	cup fruit juice or fruit-flavored liqueur
½	cup water
2	tablespoons lemon juice

or, the following may be used:

½	cup water
½	cup sugar
2	tablespoons lemon juice.

Filling

2   cups sliced fresh strawberries
or other fresh fruit thinly sliced
(Canned fruit or jam can be substituted
for the fresh fruit.)

1   cup heavy cream, whipped stiff
sugar or vanilla sugar to taste, to add
while whipping the cream

Assembly

This cake can be assembled right on the serving dish. Center the bottom layer on the serving dish. Using a pastry brush or a small spoon, moisten the bottom layer of the cake with one-half the blended liquid. The cake should not be soaked. Spread about half of the fruit on the cake. Spread half of the whipped cream on top of the fruit. Cover with the top layer. Again moisten the cake. The cake can be made ahead and stored in the refrigerator at this point to be finished the next day.

To finish the cake, cover the top layer with the remaining fruit and the whipped cream. Decorate with fresh fruits and chocolate shavings. Chill until serving time.

Three, or even more, layers may be used if desired. These are made by cutting the cake into more layers after it has been removed from the pan. Divide the filling appropriately. It may be necessary to prepare a little more fruit and whipping cream for filling more layers.

At Christmas time, another popular filling for this cake is prune cream jelly (luumukermahyytelö), one of the dessert recipes in this book. It can also be used as a frosting over the cake and then decorated with whipped cream.

Chapter Twenty-Two

How Has the Traditonal Menu Changed?

The convenience and availability of refrigeration and freezing in homes have allowed changes in modern-day food preparations. The availability of a variety of fruits and vegetables throughout the year has added new dimensions to food traditions, as well. Though the traditional Christmas Eve dinner has stayed much the same, some changes have been occurring. In the case of the rice porridge, it seems that a new tradition is developing. Guests are invited for a luncheon on Christmas Eve, and the rice porridge is served as a main dish instead of as a dessert in the evening. Also, at Christmas Eve dinner, a roasted turkey is replacing the ham as the main dish, and the turkey is served again on Christmas Day. The turkey may be stuffed with grapes and other fruits and spiced with a mixture of lemon juice, white pepper, and salt, thus differing from the traditional American-style roast turkey. One or two of the Christmas Eve casseroles are served. A red cabbage salad may be chosen to replace the Rosolli.

A Christmas Eve Menu

Lutefisk with boiled potatoes and white sauce

Roast turkey
Carrot casserole
Rutabaga casserole
Steamed green peas

Red cabbage salad

Christmas bread

Prune cream and cookies

Coffee

Liisa's Spiced Red Cabbage
Liisan maustettu punakaali

3   apples, peeled, cored, and cubed
¼   cup chopped onions
¼   cup butter
1   red cabbage (about 2 pounds), sliced very thinly
1   tablespoon sugar
1½   teaspoons salt
2   whole cloves
2   bay leaves
     dash of cinnamon
¼   cup vinegar
½   cup water

Sauté apples and onions in butter. Add the cabbage and other ingredients. Simmer 1½ hours. Serve hot. This recipe is easy to make, and it adds an interesting flavor to the menu.

A Boxing Day (*Tapanin päivä*) Menu

Smoked-fish salad

Oven-baked salmon
Boiled and peeled salad potatoes with dill
Steamed green peas

Fresh green salad

Victoria's dessert

Christmas bread

Coffee and cake

Smoked-Fish Salad
Savukala salaatti

¼ pound smoked fish (salmon or chub),
  boned and flaked
2 small potatoes, boiled, peeled, and cubed
1 tart apple, peeled, cored, and cubed
1 tablespoon chopped white onion
1 tablespoon of chopped fresh dill

Dressing

2 tablespoons rice vinegar
5 tablespoons salad oil
  dash white pepper and salt
  (Remember that the smoked fish is salted.)

Mix the salad ingredients in a bowl. Mix the dressing, shaking it well. Combine dressing with the salad ingredients. Cover and refrigerate about an hour before serving. This recipe can be served as an appetizer or as a side salad.

Oven-Baked Salmon
Uuni lohi

1   pound salmon fillet
1½ cups of white wine
½   cup of water
1   large lemon, sliced
½   teaspoon of white pepper
     fresh dill for baking and decoration

Select a baking dish to fit the size of the salmon fillet. Arrange slices of lemon on the bottom. Put the fillet, skin side down, over the lemon slices. Shake wine, water, white pepper, and salt together and pour over the fish. Cover the fillet with the rest of the lemon slices, and place sprays of dill on top. Cover the dish with aluminum foil. Bake at 375° F for about 30 minutes. When the fish flakes easily, it is ready to serve. Before bringing it to the table, replace the cooked lemon slices and the dill sprays with fresh ones.

Sauce

1   cup of sour cream
1   tablespoon homemade mustard (*See* Christmas ham with homemade mustard, page 33)
1   tablespoon fresh seedless cucumber, very finely chopped

Mix the sauce ingredients, and serve it separately with the fish.

Chapter Twenty-Three

Christmas Forever

The dark period of the Finnish winter when the daylight barely breaks over the horizon for a few hours sets the mystical background for the Christmas season. One can understand how the Christmas season has been a much-anticipated festivity for centuries for gathering families and friends together around good cooking and festive activities. On Epiphany, the 6th of January, the Christmas season ends in Finland with the holiday, *Loppiainen*. After *Loppiainen*, the tree is taken down, the decorations are put away, and everyday life continues as before the celebration. Now it is time to follow the old custom of making pea soup using the leftovers from the Christmas Eve dinner.

Pea Soup
Hernekeitto

	the left over ham bone
	(Remove and cube the meat left on the bone.)
2	cups split green peas
6	cups water
3	carrots, peeled and cut into small pieces.
	salt to taste (Do not over salt; remember the ham was salted.)
	ginger to taste
	marjoram to taste
10-12	whole white pepper corns
3-4	bay leaves

Rinse the peas. (Do not soak split peas.) In a large kettle bring the water to a boil with the peas, the carrots, the bone, and the cubed ham. Turn the burner heat to low and simmer until the carrots are soft and the pea skins pop open (2 to 3 hours). Add water if needed. Add salt, ginger, marjoram, white pepper corns, and the bay leaves. Check the seasoning. Remove the ham bone.

This is a good soup to freeze. When reheating, if the soup has thickened, just add water to get the desired consistency.

In the wonderful spirit of Christmas, an old Finnish Christmas song, *No, onkos tullut kesä,* (Oh, has the summer arrived?) ends with the words, "*oi jospa ihmisellä ois joulu ainainen.*" ("If we only had Christmas forever.") The words were written by the poet, J.H. Erkko, and the music is based on a Finnish folk tune.

Oh, has the summer arrived in the midst of the winter? Should we build a nesting place for the little birds?	*No onkos tullut kesä nyt talven keskelle, ja laitetaankos pesä myös pikkulinnuillen?*
The candles on the Christmas tree are like blossoms and brighten the dark winter nights.	*Jo kuusi kynttilöitä on käynyt kukkimaan pimeitä talven öitä näin ehkä valaistaan.*
The elderly become young and play like children, even the stooped backs straighten up and everyone is happy.	*Ja vanhakin nyt nuortuu kuin lapsi leikkimään, ja koukkuselkä suortuu niin kaikk' on mielissään.*
The warm heartfelt desire on everyone's mind - if we only had Christmas forever!	*Ja hyvä lämmin hellä on mieli jokaisen, oi jospa ihmisellä ois joulu ainainen.*

Recipe Index

Cheese
Egg cheese, 44.
Flat cheese, 46.
Juoksetejuusto, 46.
Munajuusto, 44.

Condiments
Christmas mustard, 33, 34.
Joulusinappi, 33, 34.

Cookies
Almond balls, 64.
Butter rings, 63.
Christmas ginger cookies, 60.
Cinnamon "S" cookies, 62.
Cookies for the gentry, 65.
Hazelnut cookies, 66.
Herrasväen leivät, 65.
Joulupiparkakut, 60.
Kaneli ässät, 62.
Mantelipallot, 64.
Pähkinäpyörykät, 66.
Voirinkilät, 63.

Desserts
Cranberry parfait, 56.
Karpalovaahto, 56.
Luumukermahyytelö, 55.
Luumukiisseli, 54.
Mixed fruit soup, 86.
Prune cream, 55.
Prune pudding, 54.
Rice porridge, 85.
Riisipuuro, 85.
Sekahedelmäkeitto, 86.

Victoria's dessert, 53.
Viktorian jälkiruoka, 53.

Drinks
Glög with alcohol, 80.
Glög without alcohol, 81, 82.
Homemade Beer, 10.
Koti kalja, 10.

Fish
Baked lutefisk, 28.
Baked salmon, 100.
Boiled lutefisk, 29.
Lipeäkala keitetty, 28.
Lipeäkala uunissa paistettu, 29.
Savukala salaatti, 99.
Smoke fish salad, 99.
Uuni lohi, 100.

Meat
Aino's ham with home
  made mustard, 32.
Ainon joulukinkku, 32.

Pastries
Karelian pastries, 89.
Karjalanpiirakat, 89.
Lohipiirakka, 88.
Salmon pastry, 88.

Salads
Herring salad, 22.
Maustettu punakaali, 97.
Rosolli tai sillisalaatti, 22.
Savukala salaatti, 99.
Smoked-fish salad, 99.
Spiced red cabbage, 97.

Sauce
  Valkoinen maito kastike, 29.
  White sauce, 29.
Soup
  Hernekeitto, 102.
  Pea soup, 102.

Sweets
  Kola candies, 77.
  Kola karamellit, 77.

Bibliography

Ahti, H. Heikkinen, L. Järvinen, V. and Pauloff, M. (eds.), *Entertaining the Finnish Way*, Werner Söderström Oy, Helsinki, 1982.

Karjalainen, Sirpa, *Juhlan aika* (third edition), Werner Söderström Oy, Helsinki, 1998.

Nirkko, Juha and Vento, Urpo (eds), *Joulu joutui*, Suomalaisen Kirjallisuuden Seura, Helsinki, 1993.

Oy Valitut Palat - Reader's Digest, *Sitä joulua en unohda*, Otava, Finland, 1979.

Pesonen, Olavi, *Laulukirja* (seventh edition), Valistus, Helsinki, 1947.

Tolvanen, Kirsti, *Kotikokin herkkukirja*, Werner Söderström Oy, Helsinki, 1962.

Uusivirta, Hilkka, *Suomalaisen ruokaperinteen keittokirja*, Werner Söderström Oy, Helsinki, 1982.

Valio Oy, *Tervetuloa joulu*, Yhteiskirjapaino Oy, Helsinki, 1981.

A Note about Metric Units

Most of the measurements used in this book can be changed to metric units by using the following instructions.

Cups to deciliters	Multiply cups by 2.37
Quarts to liters	Multiply quarts by .95
Ounces to grams	Multiply ounces by 28.4
Pounds to grams	Multiply pounds by 454
Pounds to kilograms	Multiply pounds by .454
Fahrenheit to Celsius	Subtract 32, then multiply by $\frac{5}{9}$

Approximates for some quantities appearing frequently in the recipes are:

AMERICAN	METRIC	AMERICAN	METRIC
½ cup	1¼ deciliter	6 ounces	180 grams
1 cup	2½ deciliters	8 ounces	235 grams
2 cups	5 deciliters		
4 cups (1 quart)	.95 liter	2 pounds	.9 kilograms
8 cups (2 quarts)	1.9 liters	6.5 pounds	3 kilograms
		170° F	77° C
1 ounce	30 grams	300° F	150° C
2 ounces	60 grams	325° F	163° C
3 ounces	90 grams	350° F	177° C
4 ounces	120 grams	375° F	190° C
		400° F	205° C